AF809652

51 Must Know Facts About Brain

BESTSELLING NON-FICTION

- Gravity by George Gamow
  Sciences/Physics, ISBN: 9789388118705
- How to Develop Self-Confi. and Pub. Speaking by Dale Carnegie
  Mind, Body & Spirit, ISBN: 9789388118286
- How to Stop Worrying and Start Living by Dale Carnegie
  Mind, Body & Spirit, ISBN: 9789387669161
- How to Win Friends and Influence People by Dale Carnegie
  Self Help/General, ISBN: 9789387669178
- Mein Kampf by Adolf Hitler
  Autobiographies/Leaders, ISBN: 9789387669260
- My Experiments with Truth by Mahatma Gandhi
  Autobiographies/Leaders, ISBN: 9789387669277
- Relativity by Albert Einstein
  Sciences/Physics, ISBN: 9789387669185
- The Art of War by Sun Tzu
  Self Help/Success, ISBN: 9789387669321
- The Diary of a Young Girl by Anne Frank
  Autobiographies/Memoirs, ISBN: 9789387669208
- The Magic of Believing by Claudie Bristol
  Religion/Christianity, ISBN: 9789388118217
- The Miracles of Your Mind by Joseph Murphy
  Mind, Body & Spirit, ISBN: 9789387669215
- The Power of Your Subconscious Mind by Joseph Murphy
  Mind, Body & Spirit, ISBN: 9789387669222
- The Richest Man in Babylon by George S. Clason
  Business & Economics, ISBN: 9789388118354
- Think and Grow Rich by Napoleon Hill
  Self Help/Success, ISBN: 9789387669352

Search the book by its ISBN

51 Must Know Facts About

BRAIN

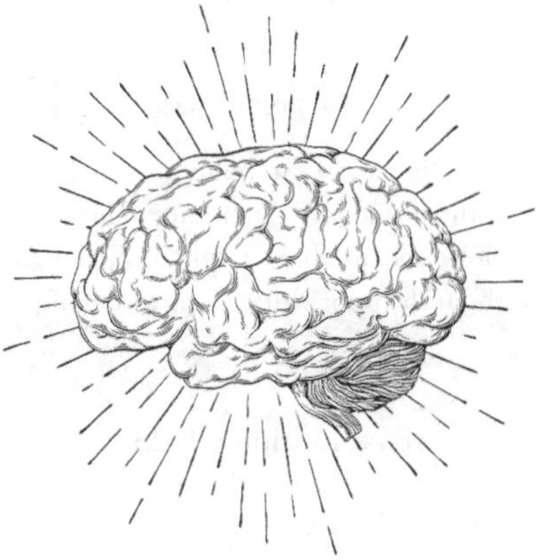

GENERAL PRESS

Published by
GENERAL PRESS
4805/24, Fourth Floor, Krishna House
Ansari Road, Daryaganj, New Delhi - 110002
Ph : 011-23282971, 45795759
E-mail : generalpressindia@gmail.com

www.generalpress.in

First Edition : 2023

ISBN : 9789354994654

Published by Azeem Ahmad Khan for General Press

Contents

Introduction

The human brain is extraordinary. It is the body's control centre. We must know how neurons work, how the brain develops, how it controls movement and perceives the senses, what happens during sleep, and how language, learning, and memory are developed. Technology is finally unlocking the secrets of the brain. It is explaining why we behave the way we do. It is helping experts develop new methods and machines to boost our brain power and it is revealing the unique capabilities we all have inside our heads.

The human brain is the command centre for the human nervous system. It receives signals from the body's sensory organs and outputs information to the muscles. The human brain has the same basic structure as other mammal brains but is larger in relation to body size than any other brains.

There are about 100 billion tiny cells in your brain called 'neurons'. There are so many that it would take you over 3,000 years to count them all. Around 77% of your brain is just water and it stops growing when you are around 25, but that doesn't mean that you have reached your intellectual peak. The adult human brain weighs about 3 pounds (1,350g). It is about 2% of the total body weight and it is the last part of your body to die.

Lively and information-packed, '51 Must Know Facts about Brain' is a must read for you to know each and every important fact about the brain.

51 MUST KNOW FACTS ABOUT BRAIN

FACT NUMBER

1

The largest section is the cerebrum and it makes up over ¾ of the brain's volume. It consists of neurons and nerve fibers that transmit information from the neurons throughout the brain and the body. The cerebrum controls the higher functions such as learning, reasoning and speech, plus senses like sight and hearing.

FACT NUMBER

2

The brain is not only the most complex organ in the human body; it is the most complex structure in the known universe. As part of the nervous system, the brain coordinates with all of the body's functions.

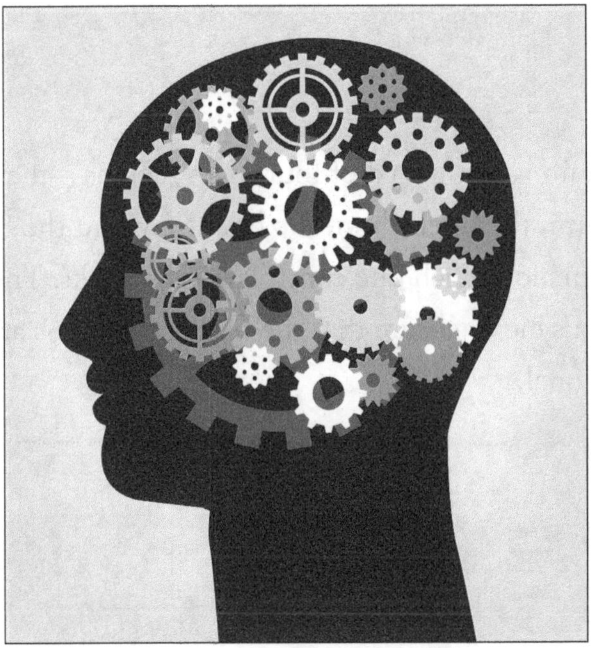

FACT NUMBER

3

The brain is comprised of four main regions—the cerebrum, the cerebellum, the brainstem and the diencephalon. Each one controls specific tasks. They work in sync to ensure that the bodily functions are fully operational.

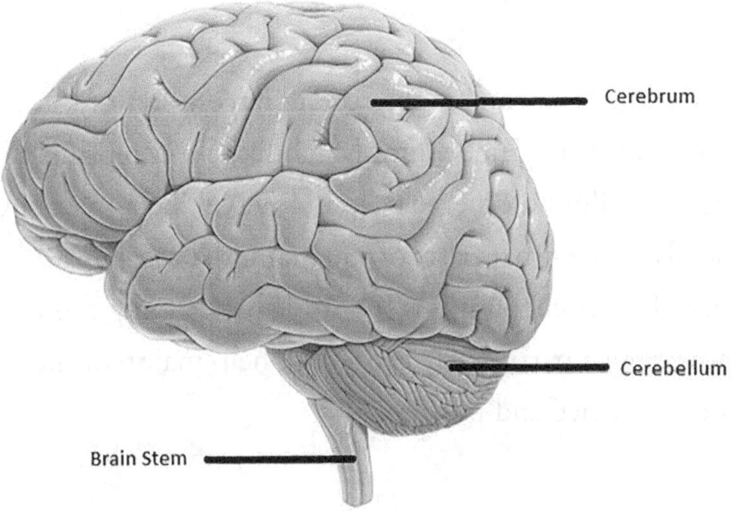
Cerebrum
Cerebellum
Brain Stem

FACT NUMBER

4

Under the cerebrum, is the second largest part of the brain called the cerebellum. Much like the cerebrum, the cerebellum has nerve cells and nerve fibers. It carries signals to the other parts of the brain and the spinal cord. The cerebellum is responsible for carrying muscle movements; particularly those that help maintain the body's balance and posture.

FACT NUMBER

5

The third region of the brain is the brainstem. It lies in front of the cerebellum and anchors the brain to the spinal cord. The brainstem is the collection of structures that include the pons—a massive nerve fibers that carries sensory information, the midbrain—region of fibers and structures that help control movement along with auditory and visual processing and the medulla oblongata—which creates motor and sensory pathways between the midbrain, the pons and the spinal cord. Altogether, the parts of the brainstem control the vital bodily functions, such as cardiac activity, respiration, digestion and sleep.

FACT NUMBER

6

The fourth region is located above the brainstem and makes up the core of the brain—the diencephalon. About the size of an apricot, the diencephalon is a grouping of several structures—the thalamus, which processes and transmit information from all senses except smell, and the hypothalamus and pituitary glands, which work together to produce and regulate neurochemicals. These structures help govern sensations, weight regulation, energy and instinctual behaviours.

FACT NUMBER

7

The brain has even evolved mechanisms to protect itself. One such mechanism is the blood-brain barrier, a semipermeable, cellular wall, that only allows specific chemicals to enter from the body's bloodstream into the brain. Despite this protection, tumours and other complications can lead to life threatening problems and diseases in the brain, such as dementia. Thankfully, scientists have found ways to improve brain health. Staying physically active and eating a balanced diet may preserve cognitive functions and even reduce the risk of developing alzimiers.

FACT NUMBER

8

The brain floats in a bath of a clear liquid called cerebral spinal fluid, which acts as a shock absorber. The brain produces half the cup of this fluid everyday!

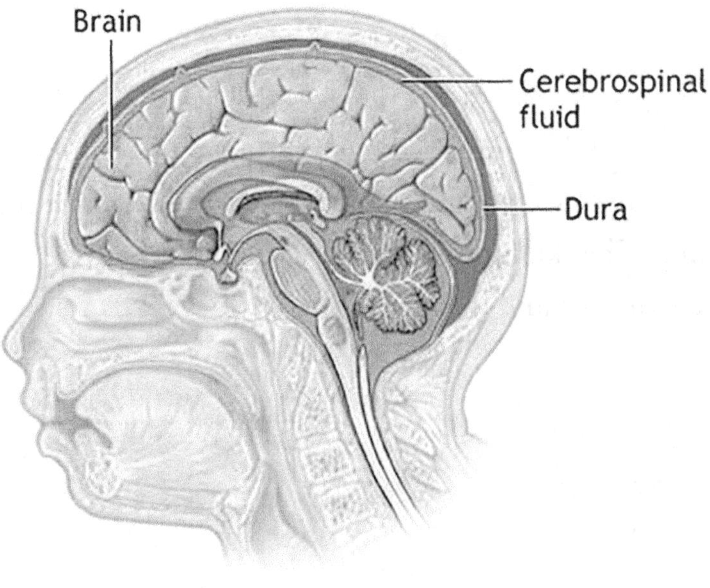
Brain
Cerebrospinal fluid
Dura

FACT NUMBER

9

The brain is surrounded by twenty-two bones, which make up the cranium—the fancy science word for the skull. The skull forms a tough and rigid protective covering around the brain.

FACT NUMBER

10

Scientific research has shown that the human brain starts remembering things from the womb. The foetus' brain development commences an extraordinary journey from the moment of conception, that results in a highly developed brain.

FACT NUMBER

11

There are about 100 billion tiny cells in our brains called 'neurons'. There are so many that it would take you over 3,000 years to count them all. Neurons develop at the rate of two hundred and fifty thousand per minute during the first trimester of pregnancy. A small piece of brain tissue, approximately 2mm in length, which is about the size of a grain of sand, contains approximately one hundred thousand neurons as well as one billion synapses.

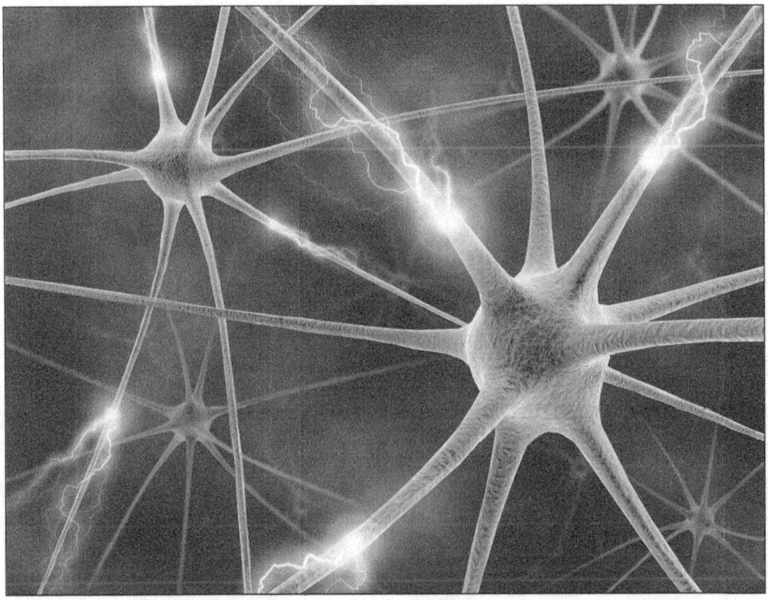

FACT NUMBER

12

The human brain is made up of 60% percent white matter and 40% percent gray matter. Gray Matter is the darker tissue of the brain and spinal cord, is made up of neurons that gather and transmit information originating in the sensory organs or in other gray matter regions. White matter is a component of the central nervous system in the brain and the superficial spinal cord. It is made up of dendrites and axons, which create the network by which neurons send signals to the rest of the body.

FACT NUMBER

13

It took 40 minutes for Supercomputer K to simulate just 1 second's worth of 1% of the activity of human brain. Despite advances in computing power, the human brain is still 30 times more powerful than the best supercomputers.

FACT NUMBER

14

77-78% of our brain is just water, 10-12% lipids, 8% protein, 1% carbs, 2% soluble organics and 1% inorganic salts. So, if you get dehydrated by more than 2%, you can suffer from a loss of cognitive skills in memory.

FACT NUMBER

15

Each minute, about 750 milliliters of blood travel through the brain.

FACT NUMBER

16

It is currently impossible to measure the possible storage potential of a brain. A rough calculation by Paul Reber, Professor of Psychology at Northwestern University suggests that if a human brain was converted into a hard drive like device, it could store 2.5 Petabytes of data. That is 2,500,000 Gigabytes. Equals more than 500,000 DVDs or 100,000 blu ray disks.

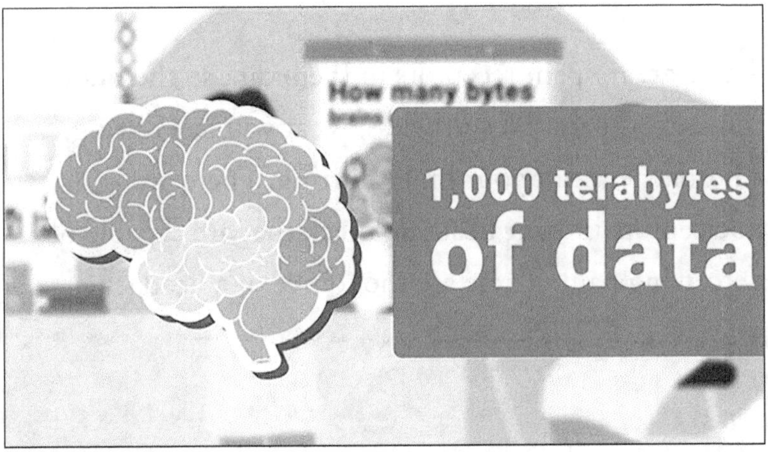
How many bytes
1,000 terabytes
of data

FACT NUMBER

17

There are no pain receptors in the brain, so the brain can feel no pain. Nevertheless, what you feel during a headache is not your brain hurting. There are nociceptors in your head and neck that are capable of perceiving pain. These are the source of a headache.

FACT NUMBER

18

The brain is the only object in the world that can contemplate itself.

FACT NUMBER

19

The brain is the last part of your body to die. After you die, it continues to work for more than 10 minutes. Moments before death, your brain receives a surge of electricity. No one knows why it happens! It also begins to lose oxygen. Even when your heart beat stops, you are conscious for about 2-20 seconds. This is because the cerebral cortex can last without oxygen.

FACT NUMBER

20

When a person is awake, his brain generates approximately 12-25 watts of electricity enough to power up a low watt bulb. More electrical impulses are generated in one day by a single human brain than by all the telephones in the world.

FACT NUMBER

21

When your brain isn't focused on a task, it switches to a default mode. You can carry so many tasks almost instinctively because you have done it so many times. Your brain doesn't need to focus on it. So whenever it can, your brain will kick into this automatic decision—making gear to save energy, freeing up your conscious mind to work on other mentally taxing things. Interestingly, we are on this autopilot mode nearly half the time. Our autopilot mode seems to run by a set of brain structures called the default mode network, which is a constellation of different areas in your brain that work together, allowing our bodies to run on autopilot.

FACT NUMBER

22

According to researchers, chronic stress changes your brain structure and functions which can lead to a multitude of mental problems. It increases the levels of a stress hormone called *cortisol*, affecting brain functions and putting you at risk for various mood disorders and mental issues such as depression and anxiety. High levels of stress hormones can stop the production of new brain cells in the part of your brain that stores memories, which can negatively affect your memory. When your head is full of stress, your brain can literally become inflamed.

anger
stress
sadness
failure
depression

FACT NUMBER

23

Who do you think has a larger brain—modern humans or our early ancestors? This discovery surprised the researchers around the world. It turns out our 10,000 year old ancestors had larger brains than we do. About 10% larger to be exact. But it is not because they were necessarily smarter than us. Several neuroscientists have explained this change in brain size. Our brains are getting smaller because our bodies are too. So, that means we have a smaller nervous system, so we can afford to carry a lighter, more efficient brain than our ancestors.

FACT NUMBER

24

Your brain stops growing when you are around 25, but that doesn't mean that you have reached your intellectual peak. Cognitive change is a lifelong process. Some skills like memory and processing speed max out at your 20's. You can excel at facial recognition and problem solving in your 30's and then gain emotional control and empathy in your 40's and 50's. A select few skills like vocabulary take even longer, peaking in your 60's and 70's. Now your brain may have matured but your mind has plenty of room to grow! That's why you should never stop learning no matter how old you get.

FACT NUMBER

25

Have you ever heard that missing one of your senses amplifies the others? Going blind or losing your hearing gives you different neurological advantages. A 2011 study found that people who are born blind develop a new way to process the world around them. They essentially began seeing through their ears. The human brain excels at adapting to difficult situations; this kind of reorganisation is called *neuroplasticity*. So when someone can't see, the brain automatically searches for a new solution. It will often rewire itself to process auditory information over visual information. It isn't quite the same as normal vision. But this work around can yield some pretty amazing results.

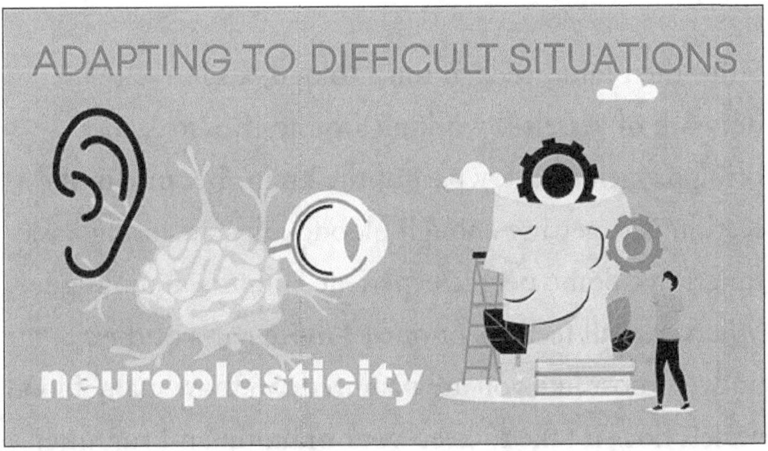
ADAPTING TO DIFFICULT SITUATIONS
neuroplasticity

FACT NUMBER

26

Since the brain needs so much blood, an intricate network of vessels is working around the clock to bring oxygen to every part of the brain. Because if one section isn't getting enough blood, you start losing basic functions. Some people experience blindness or fatigue, others lose all feelings or one or more parts of their body; almost like you are paralized. So, how many blood vessels does it take to keep your brain up and running? You would see that the average person has hundreds of miles of blood vessels inside his/her head. Your blood vessels are just so thin and tightly woven together, that they fit inside a much smaller space. Researchers are still working on counting the number of blood vessels inside the brain. However, we do know that the entire body measures upto 100,000 miles; that's like driving the widest part of the earth four times and those are the blood vessels of one average size person.

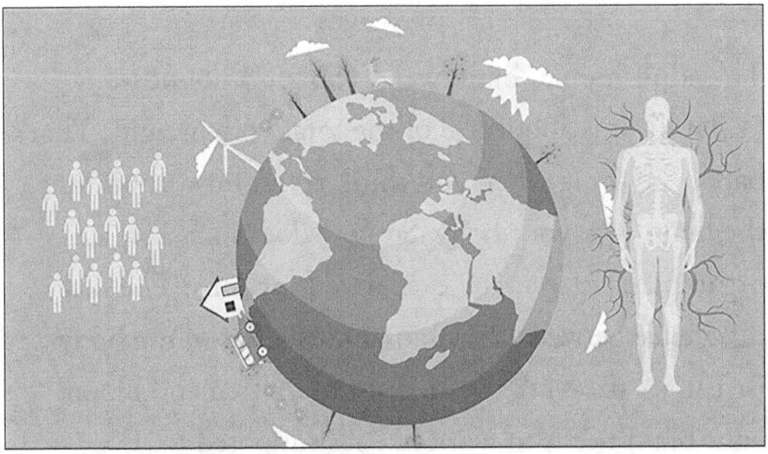

FACT NUMBER

27

The adult human brain weighs about 3 pounds (1,350g). It is about 2% of the total body weight. That's barely anything when you think about how important the brain is to your body. So how does such a small organ manage so many executive functions? The real difference between the brain and the rest of the body isn't in its size—it's the amount of oxygen and blood your brain needs to work like it's supposed to. Even though it's only 2% of your weight, it requires about 20% of your body's supply of oxygen. That's more than your entire skeletal muscles combine.

FACT NUMBER

28

You spend the majority of the day thinking. So many random thoughts pop into your head all day long. But has anyone ever tried to count them? Researchers go back and forth on the exact number. But most agreed that the average person has about 50,000 thoughts every single day! That's at least 2,100 thoughts per hour. Most of them are short and repetitive. But this goes on to show that your brain never rests.

FACT NUMBER

29

Every action in the brain starts with an electrical signal. Some are sluggish and slow. Others race across the brain clocking in over 230 miles per hour. The speed of a signal depends primarily on what kind of a signal it is. When you touch a hot surface for example, that sensation speeds through your body. It starts at the sensory receptors on your hand, passes through your spinal cord and then enters your cerebral cortex. There you perceive and process how hot the surface is, which sends a new electrical signal rushing through your brain and your body.

230 miles
per hour

FACT NUMBER

30

Your brain is actually the fattiest organ inside your body. Think about the construction of your brain. Are you picturing the hundreds and millions of neurons? The complicated network of blood vessels. The dozens of glands secreting all kinds of hormones. But did you know that 60% of your brain is just plain fat? Despite being one of the largest organs in the body, your brain doesn't have any muscle. Your body makes a lot of different things, but fat isn't one of them. So, all the fat that your brain uses for performance and repair has to come from the food you eat. This is why so many dieticians push people to consume large amounts of omega-3 fatty acids. Now those important fats facilitate brain development, save off disease and preserve your mental health.

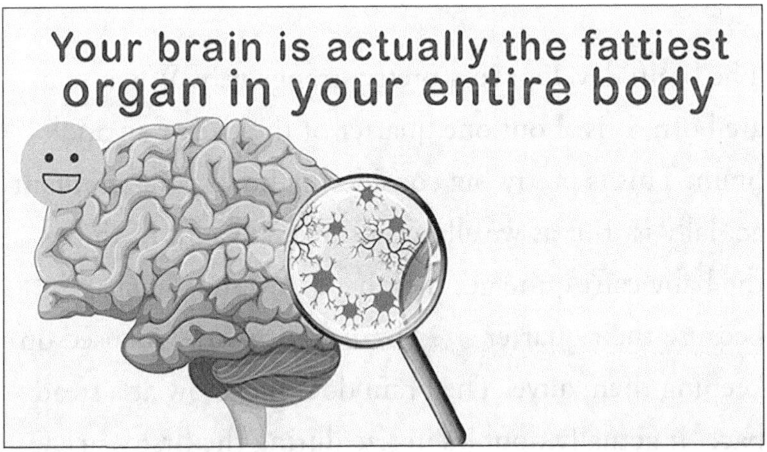
Your brain is actually the fattiest
organ in your entire body

FACT NUMBER

31

The brain develops in a pretty strange way. When you are born, it is about one quarter of the size of an adult brain. This is pretty big considering how small an infant actually is. But as we all know, there are a lot of things the baby can't quite get their heads around. That's because their quarter sized brain is primarily focused on keeping them alive. The brain does not grow at a steady pace. It actually doubles in size during the first year of life. By 3 years old, your brain is almost 80% of an adult brain. That number jumps up to 90% by the age of 5. During those crucial years, your brain is forming millions of synapses every single second. It's learning everything from symbol recognition to behavioural habits, which are important functions that you'll need later in life.

FACT NUMBER

32

When you see an image, it passes through your retina three times: firstly, as light to the receptor cells, secondly, as neural signals through the initial visual processing of the retina and thirdly, as neural signals via the optic nerve to the brain. All of these processes occur in thirteen milliseconds.

FACT NUMBER

33

Have you ever wondered why you are unable to tickle yourself? The human brain can distinguish between an unexpected external touch and your own touch, this is the reason why you can't tickle yourself.

FACT NUMBER

34

About 90 minutes after you fall asleep, you enter a stage called REM sleep. During this stage, your brain becomes highly active while your muscles become prayalyzed. Your breathing and heart rate becomes erratic. Your brain begins processing and recording information very actively, allowing you to remember what you have learned before sleeping. This is also when you start dreaming.

FACT NUMBER

35

The ability of the brain to multitask is merely an illusion. According to the researchers, less than 3% of people can efficiently do two things simultaneously. For those of you who multitask on a regular basis, all your brain is doing is going back and forth from one task to another instantaneously, creating a semblance of multitasking.

FACT NUMBER

36

The *amygdala* is recognized as a component of the limbic system and is thought to play a crucial role in processing emotions and behaviours. It has become best known for its role in fear processing. When we are exposed to a fearful stimulus, information about that stimulus is immediately sent to the *amygdala*, which can then send signals to areas of the brain like the hypothalamus to trigger a "fight or flight" response.

FACT NUMBER

37

People find it hard to maintain eye contact when talking, possibly because the dual task of maintaining eye contact while also racking the brain for a word is just too demanding, so the brain pushes for breaking eye contact to focus exclusively on finding a word that will fulfil the obligation.

FACT NUMBER

38

The reason we get more creative ideas in the shower is because such relaxing activity triggers the brain to release large amounts of *dopamine*. The more *dopamine* that is released, the more creative we are. When we have a relaxed state of mind, we are more likely to turn attention inwards, able to make insightful connections.

FACT NUMBER

39

It is a popular misconception that your brain records memories like a video. Instead, it takes snapshots of the more important pieces of the events and when you recall the event it simply guesses what happened in between based upon prior experience and generalisation

FACT NUMBER

40

After the age of twenty-five or just when you reach peak development, the brain starts to slowly shrink. Research suggests that the male brain shrinks faster than the female brain.

FACT NUMBER

41

Mirror neurons were discovered in the 1990's. It is now a growing belief of the scientific community that they are responsible for feelings of empathy. This is why when you see someone hurt himself or herself; the same pain area will light up in your brain causing you to flinch.

FACT NUMBER

42

The brain is very poor at concentrating for long periods and needs to have a break approximately every 90 minutes.

FACT NUMBER

43

With the exception of the various degenerative brain diseases, your brain never loses its ability to learn, change, and adapt to new situations. The brain is effectively plastic and is constantly rewiring itself depending upon the context.

FACT NUMBER

44

Bacteria living in the gut can remotely influence the activity of cells in the brain. The food we eat influences the ability of bacteria in our gut to produce small molecules, some of which are capable of travelling all the way to the brain. These molecules affect the activity of cells in the brain that are involved in controlling inflammation and neurodegeneration.

FACT NUMBER

45

The surgical world made its first real bit of progress in the late 18th century. Brain surgery is one of the most complicated and volatile kinds of surgery. Archaeologists found evidence that the first brain surgery happened during the stone age. Over 5,000 years ago, early humans were doing something called trepanation, it is when you remove a bone from someone's skull.

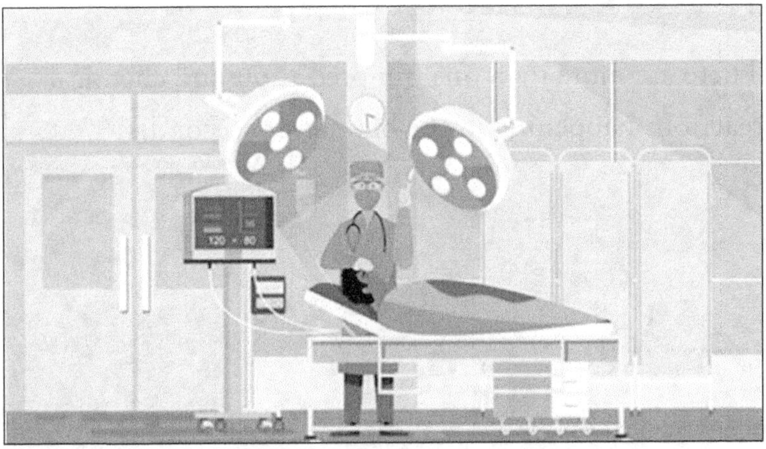
120 · 80

FACT NUMBER

46

There are more than one hundred thousand chemical reactions happening in the brain every second.

FACT NUMBER

47

When you embark on the process of learning something new or changing an old habit, you are essentially sending out positive emotions that come in the form of two hormones called *dopamine* and *serotonin*, which are released in the brain. *Dopamine* is a neurotransmitter that helps control the brain's pleasure or reward centres. *Serotonin* is a neurotransmitter, linked to tranquillity, reason, and calm. It keeps your emotions under control by helping with sleep and calming anxiety.

FACT NUMBER

48

Ever wondered why we cry when we are extremely happy and extremely sad? A specific part of the limbic brain called the hypothalamus is highly involved in processing emotions and triggers crying as a response from intense emotions whether they are positive or negative.

FACT NUMBER

49

Part of the reason why dieting is so difficult is also down to processes in your brain. When the body is deprived of food, neurons in the brain begin to cannibalize part of themselves, the process is known as *autophagy*, which literally means self eating. This provides a source of energy but also sets off hunger signals which prompt you to eat quickly.

FACT NUMBER

50

Dreaming requires more brain activity than any waking function.

FACT NUMBER

51

Your brain is constantly working to maintain a sense of continuity in your vision and perception of time, but even the slightest movement of eyes can disrupt this. Whenever you quickly move your eyes from one point of focus to another, there is a tiny disruption in your vision, which your brain fills in by forcing you to perceive the new visual scene for a split longer. This is why when you first look at an analogue clock, it appears as though the second hand takes a moment longer than a second to move.

OTHER HARDBACK BOOKS

- 1984 by George Orwell
  Fiction/Classics, ISBN: 9788193545836
- Abraham Lincoln by Lord Charnwood
  Biographies/Leaders, ISBN: 9789387669147
- Alice's Adventures in Wonderland by Lewis Carroll
  Children's/Classics, ISBN: 9789387669055
- Animal Farm by George Orwell
  Fiction/Classics, ISBN: 9789387669062
- Anthem by Ayn Rand
  Fiction/Classics, ISBN: 9789389157178
- As a Man Thinketh by James Allen
  Fiction/Classics, ISBN: 9789388118422
- Awakened Imagination by Neville Goddard
  Religion & Spirituality, ISBN: 9789389157185
- Be What You Wish by Neville Goddard
  Mind, Body & Spirit, ISBN: 9789388118163
- Becoming a Writer by Dorothea Brande
  Self Help/General, ISBN: 9789389157192
- Believe in Yourself by Joseph Murphy
  Mind, Body & Spirit, ISBN: 9789388118439
- Black Beauty by Anna Sewell
  Children's/Classics, ISBN: 9789388118262
- Civilization and Its Discontents by Sigmund Freud
  Social Sciences/General, ISBN: 9789388118279
- Demian by Hermann Hesse
  Fiction/Classics, ISBN: 9789388118170
- Feeling is the Secret by Neville Goddard
  Religion & Spirituality, ISBN: 9789389157208

Search the book by its ISBN

OTHER HARDBACK BOOKS

- Gitanjali by Rabindranath Tagore
  Fiction/Poems, ISBN: 9789387669079
- Great Speeches of Abraham Lincoln by Abraham Lincoln
  History/United States, ISBN: 9789387669154
- How to Attract Money by Joseph Murphy
  Self Help/Success, ISBN: 9789388118446
- How to be Filled with the Holy Spirit by A.W. Tozer
  Religion/Christianity, ISBN: 9789389157215
- How to Enjoy Your Life and Your Job by Dale Carnegie
  Self Help/General, ISBN: 9789388118293
- Illust. Biography of William Shakespeare by Manju Gupta
  Biographies/Authors, ISBN: 9789387669246
- Madhubala by Manju Gupta
  Biographies/Cinems, ISBN: 9789387669253
- Mansarover 1 (Hindi) by Premchand
  Fiction/Short Stories, ISBN: 9789387669086
- Meditations by Marcus Aurelius
  Non Fiction/Philosopy, ISBN: 9789388118781
- My Inventions: The Autobio. of Nikola Tesla by Nikola Tesla
  Autobiographies/Scientists, ISBN: 9789388118187
- Selected Stories of Rabindranath Tagore by Rabindranath Tagore
  Fiction/Short Stories, ISBN: 9789387669307
- Sense and Sensibility by Jane Austen
  Fiction/Classics, ISBN: 9789387669109
- Siddhartha by Hermann Hesse
  Fiction/Classics, ISBN: 9789387669116
- Tales from India by Rudyard Kipling
  Fiction/Short Stories, ISBN: 9789387669123

Search the book by its ISBN

OTHER HARDBACK BOOKS

- Tales from Shakespeare by Charles Lamb, Mary Lamb
  Fiction/Short Stories, ISBN: 9789387669314
- The Alchemy of Happiness by Al-Ghazzali
  Religion & Spirituality, ISBN: 9789388118309
- The Art of Public Speaking by Dale Carnegie
  Self Help/General, ISBN: 9789388118477
- The Autobiography of a Yogi by Paramahansa Yogananda
  Autobiographies/General, ISBN: 9789387669192
- The Dynamic Laws of Prosperity by Catherine Ponder
  Mind, Body & Spirit, ISBN: 9789388118194
- The Elements of Style by William Strunk
  Non Fiction/Skill, ISBN: 9789389157222
- The Game of Life and How to Play It by Florence Scovel Shinn
  Mind, Body & Spirit, ISBN: 9789388118316
- The Imitation of Christ by Thomas À Kempis
  Religion/Christianity, ISBN: 9789388118200
- The Jungle Book by Rudyard Kipling
  Children's/Classics, ISBN: 9789387669338
- The Knowledge of the Holy by A.W. Tozer
  Religion/Christianity, ISBN: 9789389157239
- The Light of Asia by Sir Edwin Arnold
  Fiction/Poetry, ISBN: 9789387669130
- The Magic of Faith by Joseph Murphy
  Mind, Body & Spirit, ISBN: 9789388118712
- The Origin of Species by Charles Darwin
  Sciences/Life Sciences, ISBN: 9789387669345
- The Path of Prosperity by James Allen
  Mind, Body & Spirit, ISBN: 9789388118323

Search the book by its ISBN

OTHER HARDBACK BOOKS

- The Power of Awareness by Neville Goddard
  Mind, Body & Spirit, ISBN: 9789388118330
- The Power of Concentration by Theron Q. Dumont
  Self Help/General, ISBN: 9789388118224
- The Power of Positive Thinking by Norman Vincent Peale
  Mind, Body & Spirit, ISBN: 9789388118729
- The Prophet by Kahlil Gibran
  Fiction/Classics, ISBN: 9789388118453
- The Psychopathology of Everyday Life by Sigmund Freud
  Non Fiction/Psychology, ISBN: 9789388118231
- The Pursuit of God by A.W. Tozer
  Religion/Christianity, ISBN: 9789389157246
- The Quick and Easy Way to Effec. Speaking by Dale Carnegie
  Self Help/General, ISBN: 9789388118347
- The Science of Getting Rich by Wallace D. Wattles
  Self Help/Success, ISBN: 9789387669239
- The Seven Laws of Teaching by John Milton Gregory
  Self Help/General, ISBN: 9789388118460
- The Upanishads by Swami Paramananda
  Religion/Hinduism, ISBN: 9789388118774
- The World as I See It by Albert Einstein
  Non Fiction/Philosopy, ISBN: 9789388118248
- Thought Vibration by William Walker Atkinson
  Non Fiction/Philosopy, ISBN: 9789389157253
- Wake Up and Live! by Dorothea Brande
  Mind, Body & Spirit, ISBN: 9789388118255
- Your Faith is Your Fortune by Neville Goddard
  Religion & Spirituality, ISBN: 9789389157260

Search the book by its ISBN